MW01357050

THIS SCOREBOOK BELONGS TO:

____

GAME:	DATE:

TODAY 'S PLAYERS ARE:

TOTAL SCORES ARE:

GAME: DATE:

TODAY 'S PLAYERS ARE:

TOTAL SCORES ARE:

GAME:	DATE:

TODAY 'S PLAYERS ARE:

TOTAL SCORES ARE:

GAME: DATE:

TODAY 'S PLAYERS ARE:

TOTAL SCORES ARE:

GAME:				DATE:	

TODAY 'S PLAYERS ARE:

TOTAL SCORES ARE:

GAME:				DATE:	
TODAY 'S PLAYERS ARE:					
TOTAL SCORES ARE:					

GAME: | DATE:

TODAY 'S PLAYERS ARE:

TOTAL SCORES ARE:

GAME:	DATE:

TODAY 'S PLAYERS ARE:

TOTAL SCORES ARE:

GAME:	DATE:

TODAY 'S PLAYERS ARE:

TOTAL SCORES ARE:

GAME:	DATE:

TODAY 'S PLAYERS ARE:

TOTAL SCORES ARE:

GAME:	DATE:

TODAY 'S PLAYERS ARE:

TOTAL SCORES ARE:

GAME:	DATE:

TODAY 'S PLAYERS ARE:

TOTAL SCORES ARE:

GAME: | DATE:

TODAY 'S PLAYERS ARE:

TOTAL SCORES ARE:

GAME:	DATE:

TODAY 'S PLAYERS ARE:

TOTAL SCORES ARE:

GAME:	DATE:

TODAY 'S PLAYERS ARE:

TOTAL SCORES ARE:

GAME:				DATE:	
TODAY 'S PLAYERS ARE:					
TOTAL SCORES ARE:					

GAME: | DATE:

TODAY 'S PLAYERS ARE:

TOTAL SCORES ARE:

GAME:	DATE:

TODAY 'S PLAYERS ARE:

TOTAL SCORES ARE:

GAME:				DATE:	

TODAY 'S PLAYERS ARE:

TOTAL SCORES ARE:

GAME:				DATE:	
TODAY 'S PLAYERS ARE:					
TOTAL SCORES ARE:					

GAME:				DATE:	
TODAY 'S PLAYERS ARE:					
TOTAL SCORES ARE:					

GAME:				DATE:	
TODAY 'S PLAYERS ARE:					
TOTAL SCORES ARE:					

GAME: DATE:

TODAY'S PLAYERS ARE:

TOTAL SCORES ARE:

GAME:	DATE:

TODAY 'S PLAYERS ARE:

TOTAL SCORES ARE:

GAME:	DATE:

TODAY 'S PLAYERS ARE:

TOTAL SCORES ARE:

GAME:	DATE:

TODAY 'S PLAYERS ARE:

TOTAL SCORES ARE:

GAME:	DATE:

TODAY 'S PLAYERS ARE:

TOTAL SCORES ARE:

GAME:				DATE:	
TODAY 'S PLAYERS ARE:					
TOTAL SCORES ARE:					

GAME:	DATE:

TODAY 'S PLAYERS ARE:

TOTAL SCORES ARE:

GAME:				DATE:	
TODAY 'S PLAYERS ARE:					
TOTAL SCORES ARE:					

GAME:	DATE:

TODAY 'S PLAYERS ARE:

TOTAL SCORES ARE:

GAME:	DATE:

TODAY'S PLAYERS ARE:

TOTAL SCORES ARE:

GAME:	DATE:

TODAY 'S PLAYERS ARE:

TOTAL SCORES ARE:

GAME:	DATE:

TODAY 'S PLAYERS ARE:

TOTAL SCORES ARE:

GAME:	DATE:

TODAY 'S PLAYERS ARE:

TOTAL SCORES ARE:

GAME:	DATE:

TODAY 'S PLAYERS ARE:

TOTAL SCORES ARE:

GAME:	DATE:

TODAY 'S PLAYERS ARE:

TOTAL SCORES ARE:

GAME:	DATE:

TODAY 'S PLAYERS ARE:

TOTAL SCORES ARE:

GAME:	DATE:

TODAY'S PLAYERS ARE:

TOTAL SCORES ARE:

GAME: | DATE:

TODAY 'S PLAYERS ARE:

TOTAL SCORES ARE:

GAME:				DATE:	
TODAY 'S PLAYERS ARE:					
TOTAL SCORES ARE:					

GAME:	DATE:

TODAY'S PLAYERS ARE:

TOTAL SCORES ARE:

GAME: | DATE:

TODAY'S PLAYERS ARE:

TOTAL SCORES ARE:

GAME:	DATE:

TODAY 'S PLAYERS ARE:

TOTAL SCORES ARE:

GAME:	DATE:

TODAY 'S PLAYERS ARE:

TOTAL SCORES ARE:

GAME:	DATE:

TODAY 'S PLAYERS ARE:

TOTAL SCORES ARE:

GAME:	DATE:

TODAY 'S PLAYERS ARE:

TOTAL SCORES ARE:

GAME:				DATE:	
TODAY 'S PLAYERS ARE:					
TOTAL SCORES ARE:					

GAME: DATE:

TODAY 'S PLAYERS ARE:

TOTAL SCORES ARE:

GAME:	DATE:

TODAY 'S PLAYERS ARE:

TOTAL SCORES ARE:

GAME:				DATE:	

TODAY 'S PLAYERS ARE:

TOTAL SCORES ARE:

GAME:				DATE:	
TODAY 'S PLAYERS ARE:					
TOTAL SCORES ARE:					

GAME:	DATE:

TODAY 'S PLAYERS ARE:

TOTAL SCORES ARE:

GAME:	DATE:

TODAY 'S PLAYERS ARE:

TOTAL SCORES ARE:

GAME:	DATE:

TODAY 'S PLAYERS ARE:

TOTAL SCORES ARE:

GAME: DATE:

TODAY 'S PLAYERS ARE:

TOTAL SCORES ARE:

GAME:				DATE:	
TODAY'S PLAYERS ARE:					
TOTAL SCORES ARE:					

GAME:	DATE:

TODAY 'S PLAYERS ARE:

TOTAL SCORES ARE:

GAME:	DATE:

TODAY'S PLAYERS ARE:

TOTAL SCORES ARE:

GAME:	DATE:

TODAY 'S PLAYERS ARE:

TOTAL SCORES ARE:

GAME:				DATE:	
TODAY 'S PLAYERS ARE:					
TOTAL SCORES ARE:					

GAME:	DATE:

TODAY 'S PLAYERS ARE:

TOTAL SCORES ARE:

GAME: | DATE:

TODAY 'S PLAYERS ARE:

TOTAL SCORES ARE:

GAME:	DATE:

TODAY 'S PLAYERS ARE:

TOTAL SCORES ARE:

GAME:				DATE:	
TODAY 'S PLAYERS ARE:					
TOTAL SCORES ARE:					

GAME:	DATE:

TODAY 'S PLAYERS ARE:

TOTAL SCORES ARE:

GAME:	DATE:

TODAY 'S PLAYERS ARE:

TOTAL SCORES ARE:

GAME:	DATE:

TODAY'S PLAYERS ARE:

TOTAL SCORES ARE:

GAME:	DATE:

TODAY 'S PLAYERS ARE:

TOTAL SCORES ARE:

GAME:	DATE:

TODAY 'S PLAYERS ARE:

TOTAL SCORES ARE:

GAME:	DATE:

TODAY 'S PLAYERS ARE:

TOTAL SCORES ARE:

GAME:	DATE:

TODAY 'S PLAYERS ARE:

TOTAL SCORES ARE:

GAME:				DATE:	
TODAY 'S PLAYERS ARE:					
TOTAL SCORES ARE:					

GAME:	DATE:

TODAY 'S PLAYERS ARE:

TOTAL SCORES ARE:

GAME:	DATE:

TODAY 'S PLAYERS ARE:

TOTAL SCORES ARE:

GAME:	DATE:

TODAY 'S PLAYERS ARE:

TOTAL SCORES ARE:

GAME: DATE:

TODAY'S PLAYERS ARE:

TOTAL SCORES ARE:

GAME:	DATE:

TODAY 'S PLAYERS ARE:

TOTAL SCORES ARE:

GAME:	DATE:

TODAY'S PLAYERS ARE:

TOTAL SCORES ARE:

GAME:	DATE:

TODAY 'S PLAYERS ARE:

TOTAL SCORES ARE:

GAME: DATE:

TODAY 'S PLAYERS ARE:

TOTAL SCORES ARE:

GAME:	DATE:

TODAY 'S PLAYERS ARE:

TOTAL SCORES ARE:

GAME:				DATE:	
TODAY 'S PLAYERS ARE:					
TOTAL SCORES ARE:					

GAME:	DATE:

TODAY'S PLAYERS ARE:

TOTAL SCORES ARE:

GAME:	DATE:

TODAY 'S PLAYERS ARE:

TOTAL SCORES ARE:

GAME:	DATE:

TODAY 'S PLAYERS ARE:

TOTAL SCORES ARE:

GAME:	DATE:

TODAY 'S PLAYERS ARE:

TOTAL SCORES ARE:

GAME:				DATE:	
TODAY 'S PLAYERS ARE:					
TOTAL SCORES ARE:					

GAME:	DATE:

TODAY 'S PLAYERS ARE:

TOTAL SCORES ARE:

GAME:	DATE:

TODAY 'S PLAYERS ARE:

TOTAL SCORES ARE:

GAME:	DATE:

TODAY 'S PLAYERS ARE:

TOTAL SCORES ARE:

GAME:	DATE:

TODAY 'S PLAYERS ARE:

TOTAL SCORES ARE:

GAME:	DATE:

TODAY 'S PLAYERS ARE:

TOTAL SCORES ARE:

GAME: DATE:

TODAY 'S PLAYERS ARE:

TOTAL SCORES ARE:

GAME:	DATE:

TODAY 'S PLAYERS ARE:

TOTAL SCORES ARE:

GAME:				DATE:	
TODAY 'S PLAYERS ARE:					
TOTAL SCORES ARE:					

GAME: DATE:

TODAY 'S PLAYERS ARE:

TOTAL SCORES ARE:

GAME:				DATE:	

TODAY 'S PLAYERS ARE:

TOTAL SCORES ARE:

GAME:	DATE:

TODAY 'S PLAYERS ARE:

TOTAL SCORES ARE:

GAME:				DATE:	
TODAY 'S PLAYERS ARE:					
TOTAL SCORES ARE:					

GAME:	DATE:

TODAY 'S PLAYERS ARE:

TOTAL SCORES ARE:

GAME:	DATE:

TODAY 'S PLAYERS ARE:

TOTAL SCORES ARE:

GAME:	DATE:

TODAY'S PLAYERS ARE:

TOTAL SCORES ARE:

GAME:	DATE:

TODAY 'S PLAYERS ARE:

TOTAL SCORES ARE:

GAME: | DATE:

TODAY 'S PLAYERS ARE:

TOTAL SCORES ARE:

GAME:				DATE:	
TODAY 'S PLAYERS ARE:					
TOTAL SCORES ARE:					

GAME:				DATE:	
TODAY 'S PLAYERS ARE:					
TOTAL SCORES ARE:					

GAME:	DATE:

TODAY 'S PLAYERS ARE:

TOTAL SCORES ARE:

TO HELP YOUNGER ONES ADD UP THEIR SCORES

1	2	3	4	5	6	7	8	9	10
11	12	13	14	15	16	17	18	19	20
21	22	23	24	25	26	27	28	29	30
31	32	33	34	35	36	37	38	39	40
41	42	43	44	45	46	47	48	49	50
51	52	53	54	55	56	57	58	59	60
61	62	63	64	65	66	67	68	69	70
71	72	73	74	75	76	77	78	79	80
81	82	83	84	85	86	87	88	89	90
91	92	93	94	95	96	97	98	99	100